EXTREME CAREERS

DETECTIVES

Life Investigating Crime

Nicholas Croce

the rosen publishing group's
rosen central

Published in 2003 by The Rosen Publishing Group, Inc.
29 East 21st Street, New York, NY 10010

Copyright © 2003 by The Rosen Publishing Group, Inc.

First Edition

Library of Congress Cataloging-in-Publication Data

Croce, Nicholas.
Detectives : life investigating crime / by Nicholas Croce.— 1st ed.
    p. cm. — (Extreme careers)
Summary: Explores how to prepare for and get into the field of detective work as an FBI agent, police detective, or private investigator, and looks at the daily life of one who chooses a career in criminal investigation.
Includes bibliographical references and index.
ISBN 0-8239-3796-8 (lib. bdg.)
1. Detectives—Juvenile literature. 2. Private investigators—Juvenile literature. 3. Criminal investigation—Vocational guidance—Juvenile literature. [1. Detectives. 2. Private investigators. 3. Criminal investigation—Vocational guidance. 4. Vocational guidance.] I. Title. II. Series.
HV7922 .C76 2003
363.2'023—dc21

                                        2002007451

Manufactured in the United States of America

Contents

Introduction

When you think of Sherlock Holmes, you probably envision excitement, danger, and intrigue. While Sherlock Holmes has been romanticized for popular culture, detective work is no nine-to-five job. Sure, detectives have some of the same responsibilities as people with "regular" jobs. They have to file papers and fill out reports. They even have bosses. But their jobs also put them in the middle of the nitty-gritty of criminal cases. They're the ones searching cars for fingerprints and installing wiretaps in the homes of potential drug traffickers. Detective work is definitely exciting. Why do you think so many movies, novels, and television shows have been created about the detective life?

Being a detective can be exciting, stimulating, and rewarding, but it requires a great deal of hard work and the ability to deal with pressure.

Detectives: Life Investigating Crime

Detectives have to pay a heavy price for having such thrilling responsibilities. For example, they can't expect to be home every evening in time for dinner. Investigations can run well into the late hours of the night. Also, detectives are among the first people to investigate crime scenes. These scenes are often quite gruesome and can take a toll on a person's mental state. It might be cool in the movies to investigate a crime scene, but imagine having to see these violent images day in and day out.

It's important that a person looking into detective work as a career knows what challenges they face. They should understand that to become a detective, a certain type of personality is required to endure the day-to-day reality of investigative work.

What It Takes to Be a Detective

Detective work offers a lot of excitement, but it comes with a hefty price. The work is highly stressful and most detectives meet with heavy emotional strain. Needless to say, not everyone's cut out for detective work. In order to last on the job, detectives have to have a certain set of qualities. Let's take a look at a few.

Street Smarts

If you see a parked car with its window smashed and the radio stolen, would you park your car right beside it? No, of course you wouldn't. Your street smarts tell you that if this car's radio was stolen, what's to keep yours from being stolen, too?

This is basic street smarts, which detectives use on a much more sophisticated level. Body language is an example of what a street-smart detective will keep an eye out for. When interviewing a subject— a person being investigated—detectives will ask themselves: Is the subject fidgeting? Is he or she avoiding eye contact? Is he or she sweating when being asked about the case? A subject's body

A shrewd detective will take into account someone's body language and attitude in determining if he or she is being honest, as well as gauging how much information can be extracted from someone.

language can reveal a lot about whether he or she is telling the truth.

Street smarts aren't learned in detective school or from any book. Neither can they be learned from someone explaining them. The only way street smarts can be learned is from practice. Some people would say it's an instinct. Whatever you want to call it, becoming street smart takes years of watching people, studying their actions, and understanding their motives.

Analytic Reasoning

Remember playing connect-the-dots when you were younger? The object of the game was to make a picture out of the jumble of dots by connecting them with lines. Well, detectives do something similar with their cases. They make connections between the scattered bits of evidence. However, making these connections is much harder than playing connect-the-dots! This is where analytic reasoning comes in.

Picture a scene in which there is a broken combination lock in the corner of a locker-room floor. On the other side of the room is a wallet lying open and empty. Analytic reasoning tells the detective that the wallet was probably in the locker that the broken lock was securing. Because the lock is broken, apparently by force, the detective can reason that money was probably stolen out of the wallet, too.

Most evidence detectives come across is sparse and jumbled, so they must use analytic reasoning in criminal investigations such as this in order to crack cases.

A Natural Curiosity

Which classes do you get the best grades in? Do they also happen to be the classes you're most interested in? Many people tend to do better in the subjects they find fascinating. The same goes for detectives and their cases. If a detective is curious about solving a crime, the better chance he or she has of success.

Since detective work can be draining, with long hours and irregular assignments, a natural curiosity is also important for keeping detectives active and performing well on the job. A natural curiosity will help a detective get motivated and inspired to perform well.

Good Social Skills

When detectives go under cover, they act, or play a role. Whether it is the role of a drug dealer, an auto mechanic, or a stockbroker, the part the detective plays must be convincing. This is why good social skills are important.

Let's say the role the detective is playing is that of a drug dealer—a role that is common in undercover drug investigations. The detective will pose as a drug dealer looking to make a transaction. Once the transaction takes place, he or she will then make the arrest. But to be believable, the detective has to develop a good rapport with the subject. In other words, he or she must establish a good working relationship with the subject. This subject has to believe that the detective is the character he or she is pretending to be. An undercover detective has to make the subjects trust him or her. It's good social skills that help the detective develop this relationship effectively.

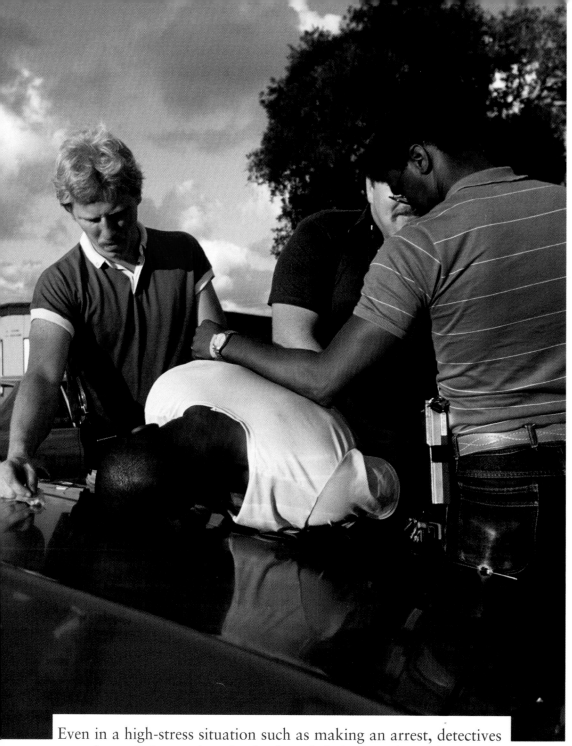

Even in a high-stress situation such as making an arrest, detectives must keep their emotions in check and their wits about them in order to keep things professional.

Keeping Emotions in Check

Being involved with graphic crime scenes, or sitting in a car for hours on end when on surveillance, can be emotionally draining in a job that requires a calm head to make rational decisions. This is why it's important that detectives have control over their emotions. If detectives become angry, upset, depressed, or bored on the job, they run the risk of fumbling their investigations or blowing their cover.

Often, in order to keep emotional control, detectives will separate their emotions from the job entirely. This is called keeping emotional distance. Some detectives have seen so many graphic crime scenes that it no longer makes them sad or disgusted. In other words, it no longer affects them emotionally. It becomes just part of the job, like filing papers or writing reports. And while this might sound heartless, it's necessary in order for the detective to keep a cool head and perform the job well.

Some detectives who have been keeping their emotional distance for years become emotionally distant in their daily lives. This is where the stereotype of the cool, emotionless detective comes from.

Harland W. Braun *(right)*, attorney for actor and murder suspect Robert Blake, waits for paperwork from Los Angeles detective Ron Ito *(center)*, who has just obtained boxes of evidence from Braun.

Persistence

In the fable "The Tortoise and the Hare" by the ancient Greek poet Aesop, a hare challenges a tortoise to a race, mocking his slowness. The race begins and the hare speeds off. Thinking he has plenty of time, the hare lies down on the roadside and takes a nap. He wakes, and then after some more running lies down again and figures he has time to take another nap. He does this several times over the course of the race as the tortoise persistently moves at his own slow and steady pace. Eventually, the hare wakes to find the tortoise now approaching the finish line. And, as the hare tries to speed to the finish line himself, he finds that he is too slow and loses to the tortoise.

This is a good lesson for detectives, considering that some cases can drag on for years or even decades. Though many cases need to be solved quickly, not all cases can be wrapped up in a timely fashion. Sometimes, the toughest ones require, more than anything else, slow and steady persistence.

Types of Detectives

Just like there are many different kinds of medical specialists, there are also many different kinds of detectives. If you have back pain, you go to a chiropractor. If you have a rash, you go to a dermatologist. If you are having foot problems, you go to a podiatrist. In the same way, detectives take on jobs that relate to their specialties. Kidnapping, bank robbery, car theft, and homicide are examples of areas detectives might specialize in. They can also focus on investigating smaller crimes, such as check forgery or petty theft. In general, detectives can be broken down into three main categories: FBI agent, police detective, and private investigator.

Atlanta police search a crime scene for evidence in connection with a pipe bomb explosion during the 1996 Olympic Games. An FBI agent and an ATF agent join in on the investigation. Investigative work draws people down a diverse number of career paths.

FBI Agents

On July 26, 1908, Attorney General Charles J. Bonaparte appointed a force of special agents to be the investigative arm of the Department of Justice. This was the beginning of the Federal Bureau of Investigation (FBI), the agency responsible for investigating crimes on the federal level—the most serious types of crimes.

Many people find the FBI to be the most exciting place for detective work because it deals with more publicized crimes than those handled by police detectives and private investigators. Terrorism, Mafia-related crimes, money laundering, drug smuggling, kidnapping, extortion, and international spying are some examples of the crimes the FBI handles.

The FBI also compiles the "ten most wanted" list—a list of the most dangerous criminals that have not been caught yet. This list has been made popular by the television show *America's Most Wanted*. Host John Walsh profiles many of the criminals featured on the list and asks for viewers' help in bringing them to justice. Citizens can also use the FBI's Web site (http://www.fbi.gov) to view the current most wanted

UNLAWFUL FLIGHT TO AVOID PROSECUTION - MURDER

NIKOLAY SOLTYS

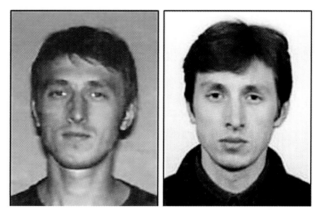

The FBI's ten most wanted list, available on the Internet, helps federal authorities solicit clues on dangerous fugitives from the public at large. Vital information on each criminal is listed on the site.

list and call in with tips. Many fugitives have been caught and brought to justice as a result of ordinary citizens recognizing them from these lists.

Starting a Career as an FBI Agent

FBI agents begin their careers by applying to the FBI office in Washington, D.C. To be eligible, applicants must have a four-year college degree and be between the ages of twenty-three and thirty-seven. Applicants must also be citizens of the United States, have good vision and hearing, be in excellent physical shape, and be able to use a firearm.

To become an FBI agent, it helps to have a unique skill, such as being able to speak two or more languages or having advanced degrees in mathematics, science, computers, or engineering. These might be needed to solve the more exotic crimes that require a language translator, someone

FBI training ensures that agents are well equipped to handle their duties. Here, FBI trainees practice disarming and arresting a suspect.

who knows how to decode an encrypted computer document, or someone who understands how a bomb can be disarmed. Many agents have backgrounds in military intelligence and air combat as well. Since these skills are so specialized, the FBI makes sure its agents are top rate.

Television and the movies have romanticized the lives of FBI agents, and as a result, many people think they work with unlimited power. This, of course, isn't the case. FBI agents are not above the law. For example, the movies might show the FBI secretly setting up miniature microphones, called bugs, in the homes of the subjects they investigate. Though they do this, the laws surrounding the use of bugs are very strict. Bugs can only be utilized in the most serious crimes such as terrorism and spying. Even then, the federal government requires that the FBI have probable cause, or solid evidence of a crime. Planting bugs without permission is a serious federal offense. So even though the FBI is one of the most powerful enforcers of the law, it's also one of the most closely monitored organizations.

Police Detectives

When there's a crime to be investigated on the local level, police detectives are usually the ones called in. You've probably seen them on television shows like *NYPD Blue.* These are the plainclothes officers (out of police uniform) who are always asking the questions and poking around crime scenes.

Their jobs take place behind the yellow police tape. They gather the facts and collect evidence for criminal cases. Some are part of what are called interagency task forces, which handle specific types of crimes like kidnapping, auto theft, or homicide. They conduct interviews, examine records, take part in surveillance, and conduct raids and arrests.

Requirements of a Police Detective

The requirements for application into a police detective program vary from state to state. Most states require applicants to be at least twenty-one years old and have no criminal record that would prevent them from carrying a firearm. Most departments also

Police detectives investigate evidence to help solve crimes. They work on the local level, usually specializing in specific types of crimes. Here, a detective looks over evidence from a case file.

require the applicant to have at least a two-year college degree, though some ask only for a high school diploma or certification from a high school equivalency test.

Most, if not all, police departments require the applicant to take a written exam. The test covers areas such as knowledge of detective equipment, the state laws and law enforcement, crime scene investigative procedures, department regulations, the court systems and court procedures, use of evidence in criminal investigations, and what constitutes illegal distribution of narcotics. The test might also require the applicant to be able to conduct laboratory procedures in investigations, understand complex laws, comprehend the science behind the evaluation of evidence, and provide testimony in a court of law.

As you can see, the requirements for the job of a police detective are quite demanding. It is rare that a person applies without any prior police experience. Most have worked in some law enforcement capacity for at least several years before deciding to apply for the detective branch of the department.

Private Investigators

Private investigators, sometimes called private eyes or PIs, can be seen as detective freelancers who are hired by citizens for specific jobs. Why doesn't a normal police detective just take care of the case? Well, private investigators usually handle situations in which there isn't enough evidence yet for the police to get involved. People hire private investigators when they feel that a crime is being or has been committed and they're looking to gather incriminating evidence.

Private investigators often work irregular hours. They also have to frequently work at night since many criminals like to commit their crimes in the darkness and silence of the late hours. The hard work can prove to be worthwhile, however. Private investigators may conduct their investigations in such ritzy places as fancy hotels and restaurants.

Pictured here is Joseph McCann, a private investigator hired to find missing Washington, D.C., intern Chandra Levy, who disappeared in 2001. In May 2002, her remains were discovered in a local park.

Examples of other cases private investigators might handle are credit card fraud, handwriting analysis (though they must be specialists in the field), investigative photography, suspected insurance fraud, and personnel background checks for businesses. A lot of these cases can be very exciting because they make each day different from the last.

Becoming a Private Eye

To become a private eye, one needs to apply for a state license. Most states require that the applicant be a certain age, usually at least eighteen years old for an unarmed investigator and twenty-one for one who will be carrying a firearm.

Most private investigators start out as apprentices at detective agencies. This is a good place to learn the ropes. There are many courses available for the average person to learn detective work, but these courses can't compare to the hands-on experience that working for an agency provides. What a person will learn in five years from a detective class, he or she might be able to learn in one year by working at an agency.

There is a drawback, however, to starting off at an agency: The new detective's first cases will not be as glamorous as he or she might have imagined. He or she will most likely be doing undercover work, such as surveillance. There is a reason for this, though. The detective has to gain experience before he or she can expect to take on major projects. As the saying goes, you have to learn to walk before you can learn to fly. After detectives learn the basics of the business, they can take on more interesting and glamorous cases.

One of the most important rules private investigators must remember is that they are not law enforcers. This means that they do not necessarily have the same legal power as police detectives or FBI agents. Think of it this way: Private investigators are basically everyday citizens who know how to gather information and evidence on people. Once they gather their evidence, they work with the police, the FBI, or some other law enforcement department in bringing a subject to justice.

Cool Tools

A carpenter needs a hammer and nails to perform his or her job. A pediatrician needs a stethoscope. A writer needs a pen. A fullback for the New York Giants needs a helmet, shoulder pads, and cleats. In the same way, a detective needs his or her tools to do the job right.

In detective work, there are many tools that can help a detective crack a case. These tools are cooler than in most other jobs. High-tech surveillance cameras, easily concealed microphones, night vision goggles, and parabolic sound amplifiers are all used to help detectives gather clues. But all detectives must remember that strict laws govern the use of most surveillance equipment.

Depending on the state, detectives may need permission from the government to spy on a subject. Some states may not even let detectives touch certain equipment. This means they have to be extra careful with surveillance, or the people being investigated might turn out to be the detectives themselves.

The Camera

To take still photographs, detectives like to use standard 35mm cameras, similar to the ones tourists use on vacation. These cameras don't stand out, so if a detective wants to blend in with the crowd, he or she can pose as a tourist or just someone who appreciates good photography. Along with 35mm cameras usually come lots of accessories: Interchangeable lenses, fast-speed film, remote shutter releases, and flash attachments all let detectives take clear, crisp shots that can turn out to be good evidence in court.

But when detectives don't want to be seen taking their photos, they use what's called a telephoto lens. The telephoto lens acts like a telescope, allowing the photographer to zoom in and out. Detectives can

A telephoto lens and other powerful camera equipment let a detective take photos of subjects without revealing his or her presence to them.

shoot from many yards away while keeping the photos as crisp and clear as if they were taken from only a few feet. This way, a detective can hide behind trees and fences during more secret investigations.

Though one picture can say a thousand words, sometimes a still photograph is just not enough. Let's say a detective is trying to catch a subject in the act of slipping a blouse in her bag at Macy's department store. A still photograph, or even a series of still photographs, might not capture the theft in enough detail for sufficient evidence. In this case, the detective would need videotape.

Microphones

It's common knowledge in the law-enforcement world that criminals love to brag about their crimes. Knowing this, how could a detective not invest in a tape recorder?

Like cameras, microphones—which can record up to twenty-five feet away—can be as small as the head of a pin. They can be hidden anywhere: in a detective's clothing, a light fixture, a telephone, a clock, etc.

Usually, the microphone is separate from the

Getting Videotape

These days, almost everybody has a camcorder. They've become so popular that detectives can carry them around and videotape almost anybody without blowing their cover.

But when the detective shouldn't be seen holding a camcorder, miniature videocameras are the tool of choice. Companies have developed technology to hide video cameras in the heads of pens and the bridges of eyeglasses. Detectives can walk into any detective surveillance equipment store, buy one of these secret video devices for a few hundred dollars, and document everything that goes on without looking suspicious or out of place.

recording device that holds the tape. Since the recording device is usually placed separately from the microphone, in a case where a detective has a mini-microphone attached to a shirt collar, there may be a wire connecting it to the recording device in his or her back pocket or taped around his or her waist. This is what they refer to in movies as "wearing a wire." These audio recordings can be used in court, but they have to first be proven to be authentic. They cannot be tampered with, and they must be audible.

Detectives go to so much trouble wearing these microphones because a recording of someone admitting to a crime can be key evidence in a case. Take the trial of crime lord John Gotti. Gotti, former head of the Gambino crime family, got the nick-name "Teflon Don" because none of the convictions the FBI brought against him ever stuck. In other words, the court lacked the evidence to find him guilty of crimes he was suspected of committing. Only after he was recorded admitting to murder and racketeering, or obtaining money by force or intimidation, was he sentenced, in 1992, to life in prison without the possibility of parole (Gotti died there in June 2002).

Undercover agents survey video monitors and listen to wiretaps during a stakeout, a job that can sometimes last for months.

Night Vision Goggles

Some criminals try to use darkness to their advantage by committing crimes at night. With night vision goggles, detectives can see up to 200 yards away on a moonless night as if it were daytime. Detectives usually use the goggles for surveillance in dark areas or at night. When detectives use night vision goggles, criminals might as well wave a flag that reads "Hey, over here. Look!"

The goggles work by picking up infrared light, which is light at the low end of the electromagnetic spectrum. The naked eye is not designed to detect this type of light, which is why we can't see in the dark. Many nocturnal animals, like owls and mice, can see infrared light, which is why they're known for their excellent night vision. It's as if these animals have night vision goggles naturally built in! One type of night vision goggles that detectives use captures the infrared light and forms a picture that human eyes are able to see.

Another type of night vision goggles uses a technology called thermal imaging. This technology detects heat instead of infrared light. Basically, it can see body heat like people see sunlight. These goggles can pick up temperatures as low as -4 degrees Fahrenheit (-20 degrees Celsius). They are so powerful that they can see the heat coming off an ice cube!

Telephone Recorders

In situations where a subject is passing information over the telephone, detectives use a microphone called a telephone control. This is a recorder that's about the size of a wallet and plugs right into the phone jack. When the receiver is picked up, the recorder switches on. When the receiver is hung up, the recorder switches off. This is a great way to gather evidence because criminals often have contacts whom they can reach only by phone to discuss the details of a crime.

Detectives must be certain that their state laws allow them to record phone conversations. Even with incriminating evidence, a detective can't use the evidence in court if the state laws don't allow for subjects to be recorded.

Polygraph (Lie Detector)

A polygraph test, or lie detector test, begins when a professional polygraph analyst, called a polygrapher, asks three rounds of questions. The first round is a set of questions that have nothing to do with the investigation. "Is Wisconsin a state?" "Does a bicycle have three wheels?" These questions are tailored to give the machine an idea of the subject's normal rates of blood pressure, perspiration, and breathing when answering yes-or-no questions.

The polygrapher then asks a set of control questions. These are phrased in a way that the answers can only be lies. This is done to see what levels the subject's blood pressure, perspiration, and breathing reach when lying.

The third and final round are the real questions. "For how many years have you been gathering information for foreign clients?" "Is it true that the

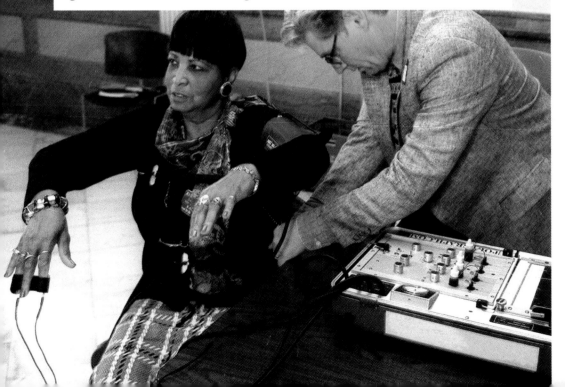

Though not foolproof, polygraph (lie detector) tests are relatively accurate in helping investigators figure out if a suspect is lying. Here, legislators in Kansas are being shown how the device is used.

name on your passport is not the name on your birth certificate?" How the subject answers these questions is studied against the previous two rounds. Based on the blood pressure, perspiration, and breathing rates, the polygrapher forms an opinion as to whether the subject is lying.

The polygrapher must also keep in mind that people can fool the machine. If the person being questioned exaggerates his or her reactions to the control questions, the results of the important questions can be skewed. However, polygraphers are trained to spot these tricks.

Parabolic Microphone

With a parabolic microphone, a detective can stand up to 300 feet away from people having a conversation and hear everything clearly. That means the detective could hear a conversation from a distance as long as a football field!

Here's how it works. A microphone is attached to the center of what looks like a miniature satellite dish. The dish, usually about the size of a dinner plate, acts like a

Fun Facts about the Lie Detector

You might remember that Wonder Woman had a magic lasso that caused those it captured to tell the truth. So is it any coincidence that the creator of Wonder Woman, William Moulton Marston, was also the inventor of the lie detector?

Since the invention of the lie detector in 1924, people have been calling it as inaccurate and unscientific as the science fiction of Marston's comic books. It is known to have a 30 percent failure rate. In fact, the name "lie detector" is misleading in itself. The machine doesn't detect lies exactly; it detects how nervous a person gets when not telling the truth, which

is only an indicator that he or she *might* be lying. Blood pressure, sweating, and rate of breathing are all measured by Marston's machine. But what if a person is so cool that he or she can lie without getting the least bit nervous? Would the lie detector actually detect the lie? Even though Marston's machine is less than accurate, it still serves as a good starting point for detectives.

catcher's mitt. But instead of baseballs, the dish catches sound waves. The concave of the dish then reflects these sound waves toward the microphone placed at the center.

This is basically the same way all satellite dishes work. The ones you see on the top of people's houses pick up television signals instead of sound waves. The ones astronomers use pick up radio waves from millions of miles in space. Who would have guessed that astronomers and detectives use pretty much the same equipment?

The only drawback of a parabolic microphone is that it's not easily concealed. But the advantages are well worth it. Detectives can record people having conversations where a normal microphone can't be placed, like outside on a street corner. This was the case when John Gotti held many of his conversations

In recent years, improved tools for sound recording have allowed detectives to hear conversations clearly from hundreds of feet away.

outdoors, believing that detectives wouldn't catch him on tape. Needless to say, they had no trouble at all recording him.

The Most Important Tool

The latest technologies and the most expensive equipment are vital to catching criminals in the act, but the most important tool a detective can have is intelligence. Remember, there are strict laws governing the use of much of this equipment. Detectives can't just go out and videotape someone or record phone conversations whenever they want to. That would be an invasion of privacy. Detectives need probable cause to use this equipment. So they must be smart and not abuse the power these cool tools give them. Otherwise, the detective might be the one being investigated by the long arm of the law.

Investigative Techniques 4

Fancy equipment is not the only way detectives collect evidence on a subject. Why spend hundreds of dollars on a high-tech microphone if a detective can get the subject to confess face to face? This is the idea behind investigative techniques. Detectives don't always have to hide behind trees or fences to gather clues. Sometimes they can get their best evidence having cocktails with their subject!

The Art of Roping

As mentioned before, criminals like to brag about their crimes. If detectives gain their trust, some criminals will go on and on about their criminal activities. Getting them started is where roping comes in.

Think of it in the way that cowboys herd cattle. They pull them into a fenced-off area and lock the gate. Roping, by the same token, is "pulling" a subject into admitting a crime, or at least into talking about a crime. And like herding cattle, roping is an art that takes years to master.

A detective might follow a suspect into a bar on the suspicion that he's behind recent criminal activity. The detective will walk in and sit down next to the subject at the bar. "Can you believe this crazy weather?" the detective might say. The goal is to strike up small talk and gain the suspect's trust, never letting the suspect believe that he or she is being investigated. The detective will then try to rope the suspect into talking about the crime.

The detective might also use a false identity, which is called a pretext. He or she might try to gain the suspect's trust by arranging a business deal or convincing the suspect that he or she is knowledgeable in the area that the crimes have been committed, like car theft for example. A detective might pose as an auto mechanic to get a subject to discuss a string of car thefts.

Utah police block traffic as they search for two murder suspects. Locating a suspect, however, is rarely as straightforward as this.

But detectives have to be careful when using a pretext. If they don't develop and learn about it beforehand, they might find themselves in a conversation about a subject in which they lack sufficient knowledge. For example, a detective must know a lot about cars to convince a subject that he or she is an auto mechanic. Not knowing about the subject at hand could blow a detective's cover. And worse, it could blow an investigation completely and even endanger the detective.

Locating a Subject

There is one thing detectives absolutely must do before any investigation can begin: They have to find the subject. This is where the locate comes in.

To conduct a locate, detectives first need to gather some information. Financial records, marital status, occupation, place of birth, friends and family, work history, and residence are pieces of information that help detectives begin to locate a subject. Detectives might also draw up a list of contacts that might have clues to the subject's whereabouts:

- landlord or realtor
- telephone company
- utility company
- bank
- employer
- driver's license bureau
- car registration bureau
- insurance company
- post office
- newspaper carrier

- local clubs or groups
- house of worship (church, synagogue, etc.)
- creditors
- magazine and newspaper publishers

These are the leads usually followed when a person moves. The landlord or realtor is obviously going to know the person has moved out of an apartment or house. The utility company will most likely know as well. The post office might have the new address. There are countless people who might have a lead.

Feeling the Pressure

Interrogations are like job interviews. Not only do detectives want to hear what their subjects have to say, they also want to see how they hold up under pressure. Many subjects will confess simply out of nervousness. And a skilled detective will know how to put the pressure on just right.

Two detectives usually conduct the interrogation. At the start, the detectives allow the subject to make a statement about the investigation. They basically want to see how much the subject is offering to tell from the get-go. They take careful notes of everything from

U.S. troops in Guantanamo, Cuba, escort a detainee captured during the war in Afghanistan to an interrogation, which they hope will yield information on possible terrorist activities.

names and places to the times of day when certain incidents occurred. They want to make sure his or her story stays the same throughout the interrogation. If the subject claims he or she was on the corner of Baker Street and Drake Avenue at 3:30 PM and later says that it was Baker Street and Easton Avenue, the detectives will spot the inconsistency and conclude that the story is probably made up.

Detectives also put the pressure on by making the subject think they know more than they really do. They sometimes have a folder full of blank papers on hand, tricking the subject into thinking it's filled with all sorts of incriminating evidence related to the case.

Detectives also keep an eye on physical characteristics like the subject's breathing, sweating, and facial color, the same characteristics the polygraph machine tests for. They can be a good start toward catching a subject in a lie.

Keeping an Eye on the Subject

Often, detectives need to watch where a subject goes on a daily basis to understand the crime they're

Video surveillance is one of the ways that detectives keep track of a subject's movements and gather clues pertinent to an investigation.

investigating. For example, someone looking to rob a bank will probably drive by it several times to get a feel for the area and escape routes. This is called scoping, or casing. With surveillance, detectives can keep a close eye on their subjects to see whether this type of activity is going on.

There are two basic types of surveillance: auto-mobile and foot. With automobile surveillance, detectives—usually two—watch a subject from their car. They'll generally park several hundred feet away, just close enough to get good photographs without raising an eyebrow of suspicion.

Usually the detectives wait for the subject to leave the area. When the subject has driven a block or two away, the detectives begin to tail, or follow. This takes skill. It's almost like a game. They have to stay far enough behind so they aren't noticed but close enough not to lose the subject in traffic. The best way to go is to follow in the lane to the right of the subject. That's their blind spot.

Another technique for tailing is called doing parallels. The idea is to not follow directly behind but drive on parallel streets. For instance, if the subject makes a right turn, the detectives will make a right turn one block down. At the upcoming intersection the detectives will slow down to see if the subject is crossing at the intersection to their left. If the subject doesn't appear, the detectives will make a left and cross the street on which the subject was originally driving. They will look both ways down the street and if they spot the subject, they'll make a right at the next street, paralleling on the other side. It may sound confusing, but this is almost a sure bet that the detectives won't be spotted.

Tailing on foot, or foot surveillance, is more risky, but also more exciting. Subjects on foot are more aware of their surroundings. They look around more. They make eye contact. Subjects who suspect they're being followed might play one of several tricks to test a detective, such as suddenly turning and walking in a different direction to see if the detective follows. They might drop a piece of paper to see if he or she picks it up to use as evidence. They might board a bus or subway and get off at the last minute to see if the detective does the same. A smart detective will catch onto this quickly and quit the surveillance in order to save his or her cover.

This all may sound like a lot to remember. Detectives use many tools and a great amount of know-how to get the job done. But the difficulty is well worth it. Helping to solve crimes is definitely dangerous, but it's also an exciting career for those who are up to the challenge.

Glossary

audible Able to be heard clearly.

bug A miniature microphone used in surveillance.

casing The process of studying an area that a person is going to rob.

cover A detective's disguise or alias.

locate The process of tracking down a subject.

parallels A method of tailing in which a detective follows a subject on parallel streets.

plainclothes Out of uniform.

pretext A false background by which a detective will gain the trust of a subject.

probable cause Enough solid evidence of a crime to warrant an investigation.

rapport A good personal or business relationship.

roping Getting a subject to admit to a crime in casual conversation.

Detectives: Life Investigating Crime

scoping The process of studying an area that a person is going to rob.

subject A person being investigated.

tailing The act of following a subject in a car or by foot for investigative purposes.

wire A microphone concealed on a person's body or clothing.

For More Information

Federal Bureau of Investigation (FBI)
J. Edgar Hoover Building
935 Pennsylvania Avenue NW
Washington, DC 20535-0001
Web site: http://www.fbi.gov

Investigative Open Network
P.O. Box 40970
Mesa, AZ 85274-0970
(480) 730-8088
Web site: http://www.investigatorsanywhere.com

Investigators of America
8221 E. 3rd Street, Suite 400
Downey, CA 90241
(562) 869-2535
Web site: http://www.investigatorsofamerica.com

National Association of Investigative Specialists
P.O. Box 33244
Austin, TX 78764
(512) 719-3595
Web site: http://www.pimall.com/nais/dir.menu.html

In Canada

Canadian Academy of Private Investigation
7172 Coach Hill Road, SW, Suite 28
Calgary, AL T3H 1C8

Investigations Canada
6-5 Scurfield Boulevard
Winnipeg, MB R3Y 1G3
Web site: http://www.investcan.com

Web Sites

Due to the changing nature of Internet links, the Rosen Publishing Group, Inc., has developed an online list of Web sites related to the subject of this book. This site is updated regularly. Please use this link to access the list:

http://www.rosenlinks.com/ec/dete/

For Further Reading

Copeland, Bill. *Private Investigation: How to Be Successful.* Mesa, AZ: Absolutely Zero Loss, Inc., 1997.

Count, E.W. *Cop Talk: True Detective Stories from the NYPD.* New York: Pocket Books, 1994.

Doyle, Sir Arthur Conan. *The Complete Sherlock Holmes: All 4 Novels and 54 Short Stories.* New York: Bantam Classics and Loveswept, 1998.

Gavin, Kevin. *The Private Investigator's Handbook.* London: Carlton, 2001.

Gourevitch, Philip. *A Cold Case.* New York: HarperCollins Publishers, 1997.

Hammett, Dashiell. *The Maltese Falcon.* New York: Vintage Books, 1992.

Maas, Peter. *Serpico.* New York: Picador USA, 2002.

Moore, Robin. *The French Connection.* London: Bloomsbury Publishing Plc., 2000.

Rachlin, Harvey. *The Making of a Detective.* New York: W.W. Norton & Co., 1995.

Bibliography

Bruno, Bob. *Serious Surveillance for the Private Investigator.* Boulder, CO: Paladin Press, 1992.

Bureau of Labor Statistics. "Private Detectives and Investigators." Retrieved February 2002 (http://www.bls.gov/oco/ocos157.htm).

Fallis, Greg, and Ruth Greenberg. *Be Your Own Detective.* New York: M. Evans and Company, Inc., 1998.

Federal Bureau of Investigation Web site. Retrieved February 2002 (http://www.fbi.gov).

Harrison, Wayne. *PI School: How to Become a Private Detective.* Boulder, CO: Paladin Press, 1991.

McCormack, William. *Life on Homicide.* New York: Stoddart, 1998.

Rachlin, Harvey. *The Making of a Detective: Five Years on the Streets With a Maverick NYPD Homicide Detective.* New York: Dell Publishing, 1995.

Scott, Robert. *The Investigator's Little Black Book 2.* Beverly Hills, CA: Crime Time Publishing Co., 1998.

Index

About the Author

Nicholas Croce is an author and editor who lives in New Jersey. He can be contacted at nicholascroce@yahoo.com.

Photo Credits

Background courtesy of the Whatcom County Sheriff's Office, Bellingham, Washington; cover, p. 8 © Gary Conner/Index Stock; p. 5 © Syracuse Newspapers/Gary Watts/The Image Works; p. 12 © Steve Starr/Corbis; p. 14 © Najlah Feanny/Corbis SABA; p. 17 © Wally McNamee/Corbis; p. 19 © Reuters NewMedia Inc./Corbis; p. 20 © Anna Clopet/Corbis; p. 23 © Grantpix/Index Stock; pp. 25, 36, 44 © AP/Wide World Photos; p. 30 © Phil Schermeister/Corbis; p. 33 © Stone/Archive/Getty Images; p. 38 © Bettmann/Corbis; p. 40 © Bob Daemmrich/The Image Works; p. 47 © Marc Serota/Reuters/Timepix; p. 49 © Tony Savino/The Image Works.

Series Design

Les Kanturek

Layout

Tahara Hasan